ST. MICHAEL'S SCHOOL,
BRIDGEPORT, CONN.

THE BUILDING OF

THE FIRST TRANSCONTINENTAL RAILROAD

THE BUILDING OF
THE FIRST
TRANSCONTINENTAL
RAILROAD

★

by ADELE NATHAN

Illustrated by EDW. A. WILSON

RANDOM HOUSE · NEW YORK

5982

CONTENTS

Something About History

"History," the dictionary says, "is a narration of facts and events, arranged chronologically."

This means that history is the story of things that happened in the order of their happening. The best kind of history is either told or written down by people who were there at the time—eye witnesses. Later on it is re-told and re-written and passed on from father to son and from generation to generation.

Many times two or three people see the same thing, but they tell about it in different ways. That's what makes history so interesting. And that's what makes history something to argue about.

The history that is in this book is mostly from the stories of different people, many of whom were on the spot when the Pacific railroad was built. Some of them were written by "Old Timers"—eye witnesses—and were published in the magazines and records of the Union Pacific and the Southern Pacific Railroad Companies. Some of them were printed in magazines and newspapers of the day. All of those I was allowed to read. Others were told me by people who had heard them from their fathers or their grandfathers. Dan Casement, General Jack's son, gave me a number of good ones. General Dodge was always making speeches and giving interviews to the papers, and Construction Engineer Reed and many other people kept diaries or wrote home about their adventures. I've been lucky enough to see many of these letters and diaries.

But there were so many people involved in the building of the Pacific railroad that there are many, many accounts of it published in books. A lot of these books are in the public library. I think you ought to go and read them. When you do read some of these books you will see that some of the same stories seem different from the way I tell them.

History is not just dates and places. It is a collection

of the things that men and women and children think and do and say, and the reports they make and the stories they tell. Everybody who writes about history has his own point of view and that's what makes the study of history so exciting.

Friends of mine interested in railroading have helped me a great deal. Among them are: Mr. Ralph Budd of the Chicago Railroad Authority, Mr. Arthur E. Stoddard, President of the Union Pacific, Mr. Wm. G. Murphy of the Union Pacific, Mr. D. L. Joslyn and Mr. K. C. Ingram of the Southern Pacific, Mr. Alan Bell of Steve Hannagan Associates, Mr. S. L. Vigilante of the New York Public Library, Mr. Daniel Hassel whose father was a railroad surveyor, Mr. Charles Fisher, President of the Railway and Locomotive Historical Society, and Mr. Milton Bernstein, Major George Fielding Eliot and Margaret S. Ernst, who love railroads.

Col. Robert Self Henry, Executive Vice President of the Association of American Railroads, read it all over for me and made many helpful suggestions. He knows all about railroads and writes books about them himself.

My friends, Lillian Gainsburgh, and Ray Rour,

* ix

Drusilla Darr and Dorothy Lindner, set it all down for me.

And two very young friends, Susan Omansky and Judy Pilpel, read the whole thing before it was really a book and told me exactly what they thought of it and what I ought to change.

Of course these are only a few of the people with whom I talked or who wrote me letters or sent me pictures and magazine articles. Anything like "The Building of the Transcontinental Railroad" is such a big subject that it takes a lot of cooperation before its history can be written.

—ADELE GUTMAN NATHAN

x *

THE BUILDING OF

THE FIRST TRANSCONTINENTAL RAILROAD

CHAPTER 1

They Talked for Twenty Years

*"Singing through the forests, buzzing o'er
the vale,*
*Bless me! This is pleasant! Riding on a
rail."*

RAIL ROADS! EVERYBODY WAS TALKING
about rail roads.

Highways made of rails—that's what they
meant by rail roads. Rail highways to take the
part of dirt highways.

The young United States had always been road-minded. Americans were always going places.

The first settlers had been travelers. After they came pouring in from Europe, the thirteen original states grew by leaps and bounds. Farm land on the narrow strip along the Atlantic Coast east of the mountains gave out. People started moving westward.

They crossed the mountains over into Ohio and Indiana and Illinois and Tennessee and Kentucky. Some went beyond the Mississippi. A few even took their lives into their hands and made the dangerous trip to Oregon territory, where the Columbia River emptied into the Pacific Ocean.

As the country grew, more and more people arrived on our shores. When Martin Van Buren became the eighth President there were four times as many American citizens as there had been when George Washington took office.

Some of them lived in the new States and the

territories. There were more than ten new States and the territories were five times as big as the thirteen original colonies.

Americans were spreading out in all directions.

Conestoga wagons drawn by six or eight big draft horses rolled over the hard dirt roads, the silver bells on their harnesses jingling gayly. Braces of mules and teams of oxen hauled wagons along turnpikes and the Great National Road built and operated by the government.

Even where the roads weren't any good, the people kept right on traveling. They traveled along the "traces"—side roads that followed old Indian trails and were hardly any more than a couple of wagon ruts.

The Conestoga Wagon

Mules lumbered along towpaths beside canals, pulling barges loaded with freight and passengers and cattle and sheep. There were many canals and most of them were built and run with State money.

However, the roads and canals didn't even begin to take care of the traffic.

Highroads of rails—that was the answer.

Rail roads wouldn't freeze in winter, turn into mud in spring and to dust in summer.

Highways of rails were easy to build. You set out two rows of granite blocks, three or four feet apart, and parallel to each other. Then you strung wooden rails—stringers, they were called —on top from block to block, fastened them down, and kept on laying more and more until the rail road was long enough. If a stringer broke you could just rip it out and put in a new one.

Once it was built a man could take a load of hay or his farm wagon down to the rail road, set it on the rails, hitch up his horse and trot off to the nearest market. The inter-city mail coaches,

6 *

even a gentleman's carriage, could use the rail roads.

A horse could pull many times the load along the smooth rails that he could on a dirt road. Passengers liked rail roads better, too, for there were no bumps or ruts to jolt and shake them.

There was no doubt about it. Rail roads were cheap to build, simple to use, easy to keep up, and comfortable to ride on. They could go anywhere and they'd be up-to-date.

People had just about started building these roads of rail for horses when George Stephenson in England invented a new contraption that people called the locomotivator. It was a steam engine with wheels. Stephenson set his locomotivator on the rails, hitched on a couple of coaches, and away it went, pulling its train behind it.

Could these steam engines on wheels—these locomotivators—take the place of horses?

People in the United States want to find out for themselves.

In Maryland, Peter Cooper built a little locomotivator—the Tom Thumb. This tiny engine went riding over the new Baltimore and Ohio Rail Road all the way from Baltimore to Ellicott's Mills—fourteen long miles. It pulled a train of two cars, most of the time going at twelve miles an hour. That was three times as fast as a good mule could pull a single boat on the wonderful Erie Canal.

After Peter Cooper's success everybody started building rail roads and buying steam locomotives. These were about the size of a modern automobile—a little one. But they had enough power to pull four or five coaches, gliding along the wooden stringers faced with smooth iron.

In New Jersey steam engines were hauling trains on the Camden and Amboy Rail Road. Down South Carolina way the "Best Friend of Charleston" was taking passengers and goods cars every single day from Charleston to Hamburg and back again.

The first locomotive in New York State was called the "DeWitt Clinton." It belonged to the

Mohawk and Hudson Rail Road Company. Its three passenger cars looked like stage coaches and were painted black and yellow.

When the "DeWitt Clinton" was ready for business, the rail road company invited a big party of ladies and gentlemen to make the trial trip. They arrived at the starting place all dressed up in their best clothes, as though they were going to a ball. Some got into the cars, and some climbed on top. Everybody cheered. The engine puffed. Then with a pull and a jerk, off they went.

The DeWitt Clinton

Before long the sparks from the engine's smokestack blew over the gay crowd. They burned the gentlemen's beaver hats and umbrellas and the ladies' lace bonnets and parasols.

Then all of a sudden the train stopped. Nothing would make it move. At last somebody brought a live horse, hitched it to the iron horse, and pulled it along until the engine started working again.

"Get a horse!" everybody yelled.

After that first trip, the "DeWitt Clinton" made regular runs all the way from Schenectady to Albany, and without a horse, too!

Whenever a train came to a hill the passengers got out and walked or drove over it. Sometimes ropes or cables would be tied to the cars and a stationary engine at the top of the hill would hoist the cars up and let them down on the other side. Another locomotive would be waiting to carry on from there.

Even the scientists were sure that if a locomotive tried to pull a train uphill over the smooth rails, the whole thing would slide right back down again.

But before long William Norris of Philadelphia built a fine locomotive called the "George Washington." "G.W." hauled a tender and a burthen car with twenty-four passengers from a standing start all the way to the top of the Belmont Plane at Fairmount, Pennsylvania. The load weighed sixteen tons, more than two times the brave little locomotive's own weight.

Steam locomotives on rails *could* go over mountains.

At once people everywhere became interested in rail roads. Companies built rail roads from nowhere, going nowhere, just to say they had a rail road. But most of the rail roads went places— from Sandusky to Cincinnati, from Chicago to Galena, up along the Juniata River, out to the Great Lakes, and even as far as the Mississippi River.

There they stopped. On the other side of the Mississippi not a single rail was laid. There weren't enough people living there to make a rail road pay.

But even so, a man wrote a letter to a paper in Wisconsin, saying that the government ought to build a rail road out to Oregon.

That's when people began talking about a Pacific rail road.

Wood Stringer and Iron Strap Rail 1830

CHAPTER 2

A New Columbus

THERE WAS NOTHING NEW ABOUT THE IDEA of crossing North America. That started long, long ago.

We all know that when Christopher Columbus set sail from Spain in 1492, he was looking for a quick way to get to the Orient. Instead, he bumped right into a new world. The people of Europe were anything but pleased when they heard that there was a big continent between them and the gold and the precious stones and

* 13

the porcelains and the silk of the Spice Islands.

At first they found it hard to give up the idea that there must be a water way from the Atlantic to the Pacific. For 150 years most of the explorers who came after Columbus were looking for a way to sail across. Balboa, Hudson, Cartier, De Soto, and many others came here looking for a great river that flowed all the way across the continent. They hoped that a ship could sail from Europe through the New World and out to the Orient, where they really wanted to go.

At last people decided to make the best of it. The only thing they could do was to sail all the way around the New World by way of Cape Horn at the tip of South America.

The New World turned out to be a pretty fine place after all. Although there were no emeralds or sapphires or pearls, there was plenty of fine farm land. In the New World there was room for a man to breathe and live in freedom.

People began to move over from Europe and

settle down here. For the next 200 years the settlers were so busy building cities and States and
even a new nation that they forgot about the
Orient.

But now that rail road building had become
so popular it was perfectly natural that a new Columbus should bring up the old idea of a short
route to the Orient.

Asa Whitney was the name of the new Columbus.

He was a New Yorker who had gone to China
on business. The trip took him almost a year for
he had to sail around the Horn on a clipper ship.
He stayed in the East two more years. When he
returned home he tried to make people understand that there ought to be a quicker way to get
to the Orient.

It was his belief that there was a lot of money
to be made in the China trade. The Americans
could make that money, he claimed, if they
would build a rail road across the United States.

Other people had thought about a Pacific rail road. The United States had a toehold on the Pacific Coast in Oregon near the mouth of the great Columbia River. Travelers who went to Oregon said that the land beyond Wisconsin—Nebraska and Montana and Wyoming and Dakota—wasn't any good for farming, but they all agreed that Oregon was a paradise.

Many people wanted the government to build a rail road to Oregon, but Asa Whitney offered to build the Pacific rail road at his own expense. All he asked from the government was a strip of that worthless land, a strip 60 miles wide, on which to lay his rails. He even offered to pay for it—ten cents an acre.

Of course we know today that such a price would have been a great bargain. Whitney's rail road would have run from St. Paul across what has become the great wheat belt of the United States. In those days people called it the Great American Desert, and on the far side of that desert there were barren impassable mountains. When you think of this, Whitney made a very good offer. It was a big gamble.

Whitney went all up and down the United States holding meetings and campaigning for his idea. People who heard him speak thought it would be a fine thing for him to build a Pacific rail road.

He took his plan to Congress. At first Congress was friendly. Senator Thomas Benton of Mis-

souri, who at first had wanted the government to build a Pacific rail road, soon came over to Whitney's side.

"At the end of the rail road," Benton thundered in the Senate hall, "we will erect a great statue of Christopher Columbus on a mountain peak. There he will stand, his hand outstretched, pointing toward the East. He will seem to say, 'There lies China. There lies India.' "

But Whitney had stirred up a hornet's nest. Rail road engineers disliked having an outsider tell them what to do. They said that his description of the rail road was flowery and impractical.

"Mr. Whitney loses his temper," wrote one engineer, "the moment someone talks about tunnels and bridges and excavations. These are certainly great annoyances in rail road construction but they are problems that have to be met."

The people who ran stage coaches knew that a rail road would put them out of business. They became Whitney's enemies, too.

But his real enemies were the shipbuilders of New England. The clipper ships were doing a boom trade sailing around the Horn. They didn't want a land route to China. It would take their business from them.

All these people had enough money to send men to Washington. There they talked to the law-makers, and tried to get Congress to do as they wanted. A group of such men is called a lobby.

"It isn't democratic," said the politicians, "for a single man to own the great transcontinental rail road. Such a project ought to be built by the government and operated for the benefit of the great American public."

Now when Whitney held meetings people were against him. Once in Philadelphia they threw stones at him.

But for ten long years Whitney didn't give up. He continued to talk about building his Pacific rail road.

Then his money gave out.

There was no Queen Isabella to pawn her jewels for this new Columbus. There was nothing more that Whitney could do.

The Pacific rail road was still in the talking stage.

CHAPTER 3

Gold!

ONE AFTERNOON IN JANUARY, 1848, JIM
Marshall came into the post office at Sutter's
Fort. This was a sleepy trading post near the
little settlement of Sacramento, California.

Two years before, the war with Mexico had
begun. While it was going on Major John Fré-
mont had marched into California and raised the
American flag.

California had then become a territory. The
Americans there wanted California to become

a State, so that they could have full citizenship in the Union.

But President Polk and the politicians in Washington wouldn't listen. They said that most of the people in California couldn't even speak English—they were Mexicans or Spaniards. Furthermore, the soil wasn't any good for farming and the place was far away and hard to reach.

When Jim Marshall came into the post office that afternoon in 1848, there was a group of men sitting around the pot-bellied stove. It was a cold, rainy afternoon and they were killing time, keeping warm and talking politics.

Cap'n John Sutter was standing behind the counter at the end of the room, sorting the mail and just listening.

When Jim Marshall opened the door, nobody even noticed him. Closing the door, he shook the rain from his broad-brimmed hat, and went over to the counter.

"Cap'n John," he whispered hoarsely.

"Well, Jim?" said the Cap'n, hardly looking

22 *

up. Jim worked for him over at Sutter's Mill.

From under the serape flung over his shoulders, Jim took a dirty little bundle and laid it on the counter.

"I think it's gold," he whispered.

This time Cap'n John looked up.

"I found it in the mill stream," Jim went on. "The fellows out there say I'm crazy, but I'm danged sure it's gold."

Quickly Cap'n John beckoned him into the back room. They opened the bundle. Inside were some shiny flakes and yellow dust.

The two men tested the stuff.

It *was* gold.

"Keep your mouth shut," said Cap'n John. "Come on out—let's see where you found it."

Jim and Cap'n John went out quietly through the front room. The men around the stove kept right on talking.

But in a month the secret was out. Who could keep such a secret?

Gold!

The whisper became a shout, the shout a roar, the roar a hullabaloo. Half the world went mad.

Americans poured into California—"Forty-niners," they were called. They headed for the streams to look for the pay dirt. Farms were deserted in Ohio, ships were left to sink in San

Francisco harbor, looms were stopped short in Massachusetts, patients were abandoned in Philadelphia,—all the young men were off to the diggings.

Before all this happened, San Francisco had been a handful of little houses perched on the side of the hills that overlook the Golden Gate. In less than a year it was a boom town of 20,000.

24 *

Miners rushed in and out of banks all day long putting their gold dust into safe keeping. Wagons lumbered up and down the muddy streets. Prospectors in serapes and high boots rode into town and tethered their horses outside of saloons. Inside they swapped nuggets for drinks. When they came out drunk, all their gold was gone. Then they rode away to dig up more nuggets.

Within two years three hundred thousand people had made the journey to California.

"Did you come the Cape around—the Isthmus across—or the mountains over?" men asked each other when they met.

These were the three routes to the gold mines. All three were long and risky. One was by clipper around South America. One was by boat to Panama—by land across the Isthmus of Panama, then up the California coast by still another boat. The last was across the Great American Desert and the Rocky Mountains, then through the alkali wastelands, and over the high Sierra Nevada.

But hurricanes sank the ships as they rounded

* 25

Cape Horn. Cholera, lurking in the damp heat of the Isthmus, killed off the travelers like flies. Savage Indians, thirst, snow and ice waited for the adventurers who crossed the continent.

Thousands of young men who had started for the promised land lay at the bottom of the broad Pacific, or were stiff and cold in the mountain passes. More were buried in the jungle, and the bones of many were bleached by the desert sun.

None of this would have happened if the people had listened to Asa Whitney. None of this would have happened if he had built a Pacific rail road.

At last, in 1853, Congress sat up and did something. A bill was passed ordering the Secretary of War to make surveys for a Pacific rail road.

Out into the unknown plains went the surveying parties of army engineers. While they mapped the land and looked for good rail road routes, they were attacked by wild animals. Some of them were scalped by Indians. Some of them were lost in the mountains and the desert. But they did the job.

They laid out five routes for a rail road across to California. It looked as though at last the Pacific rail road might be built, but the planning and surveying had taken several years.

By this time the whole United States was in a turmoil. The North and the South and the Middle West were deadlocked over slavery. States were talking about getting out of the Union. Nobody could decide where the rail road ought to start. Each section saw it as a necessity in the coming conflict. The Southerners wanted the rail road to start from New Orleans or Memphis or St. Louis. The Northerners wanted it to start from Chicago or St. Paul.

The engineers' reports were just so many pieces of paper, fought over in Congress. All the politicians said they wanted a Pacific rail road, but nobody said where it was to be.

The worst of it is that most of the surveys

could have been used. Today the Southern Pacific Railway, the Santa Fe, the Great Northern, and the Northern Pacific each follows one of these routes laid out by the army engineers in 1856.

But nothing was done about it. Years passed. California became a State. The gold mines petered out. The excitement died down. The Forty-niners drifted away. The Overland Mail and the Pony Express got to be big business.

28 *

The States were in the middle of a bloody war before a single shovelful of earth was turned for the great transcontinental rail road project.

CHAPTER 4

Abe Lincoln Picks the Spot

LATE ONE AFTERNOON IN 1859, YOUNG GREN-
ville Dodge ferried across the Missouri River
from Omaha in the Nebraska Territory to Council Bluffs, Iowa. Slowly he climbed the steep
muddy street to the Pacific House, a big frame
hotel that perched at the very top.

It was supper time. Inside the hotel Dodge
could hear the sound of talking and the clatter
of dishes. Although he was hungry, he was too

* 31

tired to face food. Before he could eat he just had to take a rest.

Stopping at the front porch, he sat down on the low stoop, laid his surveyor's knapsack beside him, and leaned back against one of the square wooden pillars. In this comfortable position, he fanned himself with his broad-brimmed felt hat.

He was "dead beat."

The air was very clear over the prairie and Dodge could see across it almost to the horizon.

Down below him, the ferries were still going back and forth across the "Big Muddy," as the Missouri was called. All kinds of boats were using the river highway—flat bottoms and rafts, a rowboat or two, and a couple of side-wheelers. Every one of them was crowded with horses and mules and wagons and people, and an even bigger crowd stood on the shore, waiting to be ferried over.

Over on the Nebraska side, 'way up at the top of the bluff, was the town of Omaha. It was the jumping-off place for wagon trains going

32 *

west. From there, they followed the Platte River trail to the Rockies. It was the starting point for the Overland Mail Coach to California.

"Town looks like a handful of matchboxes," thought Dodge, staring across to where Omaha was perched.

Out beyond Omaha, moving along the flat yellow clay banks of the Platte River all the way to the horizon, there was a regular parade of more wagons and cattle and men walking and riding.

They were all going west.

They'd keep on moving till night came down. Then their campfires would stretch out—a chain of lights across the prairie under the big open starry sky.

As Dodge rested, a man came out of the hotel behind him. The stranger leaned against one of the pillars and watched the wagon trains.

"Looks like the whole United States is on the move," he said after a while.

Dodge looked up. The stranger was a big fellow, over six feet tall and bony. His eyes were set deep in his clean-shaven face. Dodge thought he was somewhere in the fifties.

"Looks like everybody has the same idea," the man went on in a drawling nasal voice. "I've just come up river from St. Jo and it's the same everywhere."

"It's like that all the way out to the Black Hills," said Dodge. "I've just come back."

The tall stranger folded himself up like a jackknife and sat down on the stoop next to Dodge.

"Surveyor, ain't you?" he asked.

Dodge nodded.

"I thought so from your get-up," said the stranger. "I'm a lawyer. When I get dressed up in this plug hat and Prince Albert coat, I'm my wife's idea of a legal man."

"Is the court sitting here?" asked Dodge.

"No," said the man. "It's at Rock Island. Just been trying a case there. My fee was paid in part with a parcel of property at Council Bluffs.

36 *

Thought I'd run up and have a look at it."

"Land case?" asked Dodge.

"Rail road case," said the lawyer. "The rail road built a bridge across the Mississippi. Steamboat companies claimed bridge got in the way of river traffic. The bridge was burned when they backed an old boat into it accidentally on purpose. Thought they could stop bridge building."

"A bridge ought to have been built across the Mississippi long ago," said Dodge.

"Court thought so too," said the lawyer. "Ruled that east-west traffic across the country might get to be just as important as north-south. From the looks of things down there, there's a good many people agreeing with the court."

"It's the biggest peaceful migration in history." That's what Dodge had been thinking to himself. Now he said it out loud.

"Interested in rail roads, ain't you?" said the lawyer, stretching out his long legs.

Dodge was startled. He'd been out to the

Black Hills making a rail road survey for his employers, Farnham and Dunham, but it was a secret. No one was supposed to know what he had been doing. It wouldn't do to have this stranger find out.

"You been out surveying for a rail road?" asked the big man. He started whittling a tooth-pick.

This was a leading question but Dodge managed to get around it.

"Been making a road map," he said. He reached into his surveyor's knapsack, took out a piece of paper, and spread it out on the floor next to him. "For the wagon trains," he added. "On this map I have marked all the places where rivers will have to be forded, where there are water and wood, buffalo for meat, and forts along the way."

"How's it farther on?" The lawyer finished whittling his toothpick and started chewing.

"First rate," said Dodge. "This is a good trail. First the buffalo took it, then the Indians. The

Mormons started right here in Omaha in 1847, and they got there all right."

"So you figure a train'd get there too, huh?"

"Not one of those little no-'count trains they run west of Chicago," said Dodge. "But a fine modern locomotive like they have back east could make it with no trouble."

"I was down in Washington a couple of years back," said the lawyer. "Took the wife and young ones down to Cape May, New Jersey. We went in a mighty fancy train all diked out like a lady's parlor. Plush seats and soft springs and big shiny spittoons. Not much like the trains we got in Illinois. That the kind of train you want to put on your rail road?"

"That's it," said Dodge.

"Ain't much use running that kind of train just from Omaha to the Black Hills," said the Illinois man. "Ain't enough people out there to use it."

"That's just the beginning," said Dodge. "It ought to go all the way to California."

"So you're a Pacific Rail Road man?" the lawyer asked.

"Omaha to the California border," said Dodge, still not answering the question directly. "It ought to be built and that's the way it ought to go. This spot, right here where we're sitting, ought to be the beginning of the Pacific Rail Road."

"That'd be good for me," said the lawyer. "There'd be a land boom and my property would be worth something. Think I'd better go and take a look at it." He stood up. "What's your name, young fellow? I want to remember it. Just in case I ever meet anybody who wants to build that rail road."

"Grenville Dodge," said the young surveyor.

"Pleased to meet you, Mr. Dodge." The Illinois man took Dodge's hand in his own big hairy one.

Then his long legs took him off up the muddy street. He was out of sight before Dodge could say another word.

40 *

Dodge had grown excited as he spoke of the rail road. Now, as he cooled off, he knew he'd done too much talking.

"A lawyer, all right," he said to himself. "Gets a witness to talk whether he wants to or not."

Suddenly he remembered that he had eaten no supper. He stood up and started walking towards the hotel door. Then he laughed to himself a little bit.

"He's a good lawyer. He pumped me good. Yes, sir, he sure shelled my woods."

Then Dodge stopped short. "By cracky," he said out loud. "He never even told me his name. I wonder who in thunder he is."

CHAPTER 5

To Make a More Perfect Union

THE YEAR 1861 WAS AN UNHAPPY ONE. IT looked as though the Union were breaking up.

South Carolina, Florida, Mississippi, Alabama, Georgia, Louisiana, Texas, Arkansas, North Carolina, and Tennessee had all seceded.

Virginia split in two. Western Virginia stayed in the Union. But Eastern Virginia joined her sister Southern states to form the Confederate States of America.

Many fine Southern men who had been in

the United States government took the side of their own states. Jefferson Davis, United States Secretary of War when the Pacific railroad surveys were made, now became President of the new Confederate States of America.

For a few months men in Congress argued back and forth. Then right in the middle of the argument the Confederates fired the first shot on Fort Sumter.

The shooting war was on. At first the South won most of the battles.

Because of its success, the Confederacy claimed it would soon reach to the Amazon in South America. They invited all the Western states to join with them in their fight against the Federal government.

While all this was going on, Abe Lincoln sat in the White House. He had sent troops into Maryland and Kentucky and Tennessee and Missouri and Kansas, hoping that those border states could be kept in the Union.

But what about California? Lincoln couldn't

send an army to California. It was too far away, and he couldn't spare the men. He had to find some other way to keep California on the Federal side.

He made up his mind to start building the great Pacific railroad.

It would take a great deal of money to build that Pacific railroad—millions of dollars. The United States didn't have that much cash to spare while it was paying for a war, but it did have something that was just as good as cash.

Government land—that's what the Union had —land that stretched all the way from Missouri to the California border. There were only about two people living on every square mile. All the rest was public land.

When Lincoln had been running for President on the new Republican ticket, he had promised to introduce an important bill into Congress. His bill would permit any man who wanted to settle on government land to get a parcel of it. This was called homesteading.

"Vote yourself a farm," had been a Republican slogan.

The government wanted to fill up that land with people loyal to the Union. Right at this moment Congress was working on the Homestead Act.

But even after the Homesteaders had got their one hundred and sixty acres each, there would be a lot of land left over.

Lincoln remembered Asa Whitney's plan. He decided that this left-over land should be given to people who would promise to build a Pacific railroad. Now the President sat at his desk with the Army railroad surveys made in the 1850's spread out in front of him. He had spoken to many people about them and had made up his mind that not one of the surveys was right. The Southern routes couldn't be used because of the war. The others were too far north.

Sitting back in his chair, Lincoln thought about all the people going west. He remembered seeing them with his own eyes that warm evening in Council Bluffs.

And then he remembered the young surveyor —the young surveyor who had mapped out a central route for the Pacific railroad.

Lincoln thought a minute. Then he called his secretary and told him to send for Grenville Dodge.

At that moment Dodge was down in Mississippi. He was an officer in the Union Army.

A few days later, Dodge was handed an order from General Grant. It said, "Report to the White House."

Dodge was worried. Had he done something wrong?

In three days he was in Washington in the White House.

Then Dodge was in for a surprise.

You have probably guessed the name of the man whom Dodge had met at the Pacific House. But Dodge himself had never known it until this moment. That tall lanky lawyer was Abraham Lincoln. He had become the President of the United States.

The President held out his hand.

"Sit down, Mr. Dodge," he said.

Once more Lawyer Lincoln asked leading questions. Once more he pumped Dodge and "shelled his woods." But this time Dodge was glad to give his answers. He knew how important it was to tie the western lands to the Union with bands of iron and he was proud to be able to help.

At last the President stood up. He went to a map hanging on the wall and put his finger on the spot.

"Omaha to the California border," he said. "That will be the route of the transcontinental railroad."

More planning would have to be done, more surveys made.

Connecting railroads would have to be built from the Mississippi to the Missouri and from

Sacramento to the California border. But the great Pacific railroad, the railroad across the American Desert and the Rocky Mountains,

really began in earnest that day in the White House.

Dodge asked only one question. "Will the government build this railroad?"

"That is impossible at this time," said Abraham Lincoln. "The government is engaged in a war. We have neither the time nor the money nor the men to spare. The Pacific railroad must be built by patriotic private citizens."

What the President decided made history.

From that day to this, the policy of the United States has been to have our railroads privately built and operated.

CHAPTER 6

We Have Drawn the Elephant"

Now LET US GO BACK A LITTLE AND FIND out what had been happening in the booming new State of California.

So many treasure seekers had gone looking for gold in the streams and on the river banks that before long there wasn't any more gold dust and there weren't any more nuggets lying around to be picked up. That was the end of placer mining, as that kind of mining was called.

There was still gold in the veins that ran

* 51

into the mountains. This had to be dug out not with pick and shovel but with complicated machines.

Gold mining in California became big business.

Of course all the old prospectors didn't give up. Some kept on wandering around, looking for a big strike and picking up a handful of gold dust here and there.

But most of the Forty-niners settled down and looked for another way to make a living. It wasn't long before they discovered that California was a wonderful place for raising things. They sent for their families, and the population of California grew bigger and bigger.

After a little while gold and silver were discovered in Nevada. There was another gold rush.

Very few of the Forty-niners went rushing out to the new diggings, for they had been cured of the gold fever. Instead, they stayed right on their farms and in their stores, and made money selling produce and mining tools to the new crop of gold hunters.

In 1854 California was doing so much business with Nevada that a group of men in Sacramento decided to build a railroad from their town up toward the new diggings. There were no railroads in California at that time. The men in Sacramento couldn't even find a single railroad engineer on the Pacific Coast. They had to send for one from the East.

The name of this railroad engineer was Theodore Dehone Judah. Judah was a stocky, dark, very serious man. Though he was only twenty-eight years old he had a big black beard. He tried to make himself look older.

Judah had worked as a construction engineer on railroads in New York and Massachusetts, Vermont and Connecticut. He knew railroading from A to Z.

He had heard about Asa Whitney's idea for a Pacific railroad. "That Pacific railroad is going to be built," Judah said to his wife, "and I'm going to have something to do with it."

The minute Judah landed in Sacramento he began talking about building a transcontinental railroad. He wanted to start it in California and work eastward.

People in California were used to men "striking it rich" over night. They were also used to crackpots with strange ideas. But Judah's plan was just too big and too strange, even for Californians. Children ran after him on the street shouting and laughing. They called him "Crazy Judah."

None of this stopped Judah. He continued to talk.

He talked so well that before long some men in San Francisco also caught the Pacific railroad disease. About a hundred of them got together in a big hall and held a Pacific Railroad Convention. They asked Judah to address them at length.

Judah was a good railroad engineer. When he

54 *

talked to the Convention, he spoke about mountain grades, and the direction of the rivers, bridges, and tunnels. He remembered Whitney's mistakes so he had a practical plan all ready to lay before his listeners.

The men at the Pacific Railroad Convention agreed that there ought to be a railroad. They passed a lot of resolutions—but they didn't seem willing to give up any of their own money. They said Judah certainly ought to go to Washington to see whether he could get any money from Congress. Of course he would have to pay for his trip.

Judah went East. He was a one-man lobby for the Pacific railroad. Not many people were interested in what he had to say; they were too busy talking and arguing about secession and slavery. The Pacific railroad would just have to wait.

Back went Judah to California. Now everybody ran away from "Crazy Judah." They wouldn't look at his maps, or his estimates, or his pictures. They just dodged around the corner when they saw him coming.

Judah didn't give up. He left San Francisco and took the night boat up to Sacramento. There he started his campaign all over again.

At that time in Sacramento there lived two Forty-niners—Collis P. Huntington and Mark Hopkins. Huntington and Hopkins owned a hardware store. It was so large that it ran through a whole block and spilled out onto the sidewalk.

Over the hardware store there was a big room in which the people of Sacramento often held gatherings. So when Judah came along talking about the Pacific railroad, Huntington let him use the upstairs room for a meeting.

Not many people went to the meeting in the upstairs room—just a few small-town business men—but on that night the Central Pacific Railroad Company really got under way.

Judah came out of that room with promises of enough money to make a survey for the best railroad route up over the Sierra Nevada.

Judah rushed home after the meeting. His wife Anna was waiting for him in the little boarding house in the middle of the town where they were staying.

"Look out of your bedroom window tomor-

row, Anna," said Judah excitedly. "I'm going to start the survey for the Pacific railroad right in front of this house."

At the meeting four men had given Judah promises of money to make his survey. One was Leland Stanford, a grocer who was running for Governor. He was the most impressive. One was Charles P. Crocker, who owned a general store where he sold calico and piece goods and household wares. Crocker was the most energetic. The other two were Hopkins and Huntington. Hopkins was the best bookkeeper, but Huntington was the smartest of them all.

These men called themselves "The Four Associates." They are the people who, in the end, really built the Central Pacific Railroad.

In 1862 the Associates sent Judah to Washington, with his completed survey.

The Union forces had just lost the Battle of Bull Run that took place not very far from Washington. Many of the Congressmen and the Senators who had gone down to watch the fighting turned their backs on the Confederates and ran right along with the Federal troops. No doubt about it—they were really frightened.

This time Judah didn't have any trouble in making Congress listen to him.

He wasn't the only man talking Pacific railroad in Washington now. There was a big railroad lobby. Judah got along fine with some of them, especially Representative Oakes Ames and a Mr. Dix and a Dr. Durant, who represented the Union Pacific Railroad. They wanted to build the railroad westward to meet the Central Pacific.

The Railroad Bill was passed by Congress. President Lincoln signed it. It became a law.

Union Pacific men got the contract to build from Omaha west.

The Central Pacific was to build from Sacramento to the California border or until it met the Union Pacific coming west.

Theodore Judah had put across his crazy idea. A Pacific railroad was going to be built and he was going to have something to do with it. He had won.

Telegraph wires had just been strung across the continent. By means of these wires, a message was flashed to the Associates in Sacramento:

"We have drawn the Elephant. Now let us see if we can harness him."

CHAPTER 7

From Sea to Shining Sea

IF TWO RAILROAD COMPANIES TWO THOUSAND
miles apart start across the continent building
toward each other, what happens? This isn't a
problem that you can easily work out with a
paper and pencil.

The Union Pacific and the Central Pacific
found the answer, but they had to go out into the
wilderness to get it.

The railroad men of those days had a song—
"Root, hog, or die," and that is what the Union
Pacific and the Central Pacific had to do. They

had to root—or dig—for facts, root for supplies, and root for men.

Out in California there was plenty of wood for railroad ties, or "sleepers," as they were called, and plenty of rock for ballast, but there wasn't any iron.

Every nail and screw and bolt and pick and shovel had to be loaded on boats back in the East. Long iron rails, big cars with iron wheels, heavy locomotives—almost every single thing needed for building the Central Pacific Railroad —was then shipped across the Isthmus or around Cape Horn.

On the Union Pacific side it was just as bad. About three thousand railroad ties were needed for every mile of rail laid. But there wasn't any wood in that part of the country.

Platoons of lumberjacks went down along the Mississippi or out to the Black Hills to cut the ties for the Union Pacific. Regiments of laborers loaded them on fleets of wagons to be pulled up to Omaha by a whole division of horses and mules.

Shipping locomotives around the Horn was just play compared to getting supplies to Omaha.

When they started building the Union Pacific at Omaha, not a single Eastern railroad had reached Council Bluffs, which is just across the Missouri River from Omaha. One railroad got as far as the Missouri but it stopped at St. Jo, more than one hundred miles south of Council Bluffs and Omaha. From St. Jo, all travel was up the river.

The only bridge across the Mississippi was still the Rock Island Bridge about which Abe Lincoln had fought his case years before. And that bridge was too far away to be of any help.

So all the cars, locomotives, and rails to be used for the Union Pacific had to be ferried across the Mississippi and the Missouri. Then they were toted across country. You couldn't drag a big engine or a train of cars over the rough

* 63

prairies even with a 20-horse hitch. Every engine and car had to be taken apart, packed, and shipped. The parts were put together again when they reached Omaha.

After a while big shops were built at Omaha to take care of this work. But the thousands of bricks and nails, the wood, floors, and shingles needed for the shops were brought to Omaha by boat.

Getting ready to build the transcontinental railroad was hard work, but building the railroad was even harder.

The railroad men had to think of how they were to blast their way through mountains, over plains, in and out of forests and deserts and sagebrush. They had to fight Indians and grasshoppers and lizards and landslides, and just pure human cussedness. They had to shoot their way through huge stampedes of buffalo that came thundering along like armies of tanks and ran over everything in their paths.

It took a lot of imagination and courage to build the transcontinental railroad. The men who did it were real national heroes.

But there's another side to the story. It has to do with money. This was a big operation too, but it wasn't heroic.

When Congress passed the Pacific Railroad Act, it gave a lot of valuable government land to the railroad companies. It also loaned them money.

But the "patriotic private citizens," as Abraham Lincoln called them, who built the railroad, were not satisfied. They thought up all sorts of ways to get more money. They paid themselves big bonuses for doing the very thing that they were supposed to do—build a transcontinental railroad.

The Associates and many of the officers of the Union Pacific made huge fortunes. Congressmen accepted bribes and even the Senators and the Vice-President got their share.

The whole mess fell apart at last, as it was bound to do. A great many important people lost their good names and a great many stockholders lost their money. Even the government of the United States had to wait a long time before the railroads paid back what they owed it.

Only the Associates and a few officers of the Union Pacific were able to keep the fortunes they had made.

Of course many of the things that were done in those days don't seem honest to us today. It was a time when Americans admired people who made money and didn't care too much how they got it. Mark Twain, the great American writer who lived at that time, tells how everything was imitation gold and had a glittering false front. He called it "The Gilded Age."

A man who acquired a great fortune was thought to be a smart fellow and everybody looked up to him.

Theodore Roosevelt was the first president who stood up to the Robber Barons, as these newly rich men were called. He made Americans realize that money isn't everything.

Perhaps, while the transcontinental railroad was being built, Americans were too busy to notice how some men were making their money.

* 67

The people of this country were thrilled and excited at the idea of a railroad from ocean to ocean.

At that time, great things were going on in other countries, too. The English pushed through the Suez Canal in Egypt. The French were working on a canal across the Isthmus of Panama. Russia was building a railroad across Siberia.

But none of these things was as big an undertaking as the great Pacific Railroad. The railroad pierced the wilderness, opened up the West and changed the whole face of America.

CHAPTER 8

Lay Down the Iron Rail

*"The great Pacific Railroad from California hail
Bring on the locomotive, lay down the iron
rail."*

THAT'S WHAT EVERYBODY WAS SINGING THE
day they began building the Central Pacific
Railroad.

On January 8th, 1863, just six days after
President Lincoln issued the Emancipation
Proclamation, the first shovelful of earth was
turned in Sacramento.

* 71

The town decided to take the day off. Every store in Sacramento was draped in bunting and every saloon was open. The rain came down in bucketsful, and the streets were ankle deep in mud. But Californians loved a show and they weren't going to let a little thing like the weather keep them from having a rip-roaring holiday.

Along about the middle of the morning there was a fine parade through the center of town. First came the local brass band in red-and-gold coats playing patriotic airs. It was followed by a long line of carriages decked out with American flags.

The carriages were filled with California's leading men, dressed in high silk hats and Prince Albert coats. Chief among them was Leland Stanford, who had just been elected governor of the state of California.

The men in the carriages tipped their hats and bowed and smiled right and left, and the crowds along the route cheered and waved flags. Every-

72 *

body had forgotten the rain. It was as good as a circus.

Down the muddy streets went the parade, down to the levee where the boats came in. A gaudy platform had been erected, almost at the very spot where Judah had started his survey so many years before.

There the parade stopped. Those who had ridden in the carriages got out and picked their way gingerly through the mud to the platform.

In the very front row on the platform sat Stanford, Hopkins, and Crocker. They had appointed themselves President, Treasurer, and Chief of Construction of the Central Pacific Railroad Company. Huntington, the Vice President, was not there. He was still in Washington.

The people of California had already begun to speak of these men as "The Big Four."

Charles Crocker was master of ceremonies on this great day. He really looked the part. He was a tall man and weighed more than 240 pounds. His face shone above a flowing goatee.

As he stepped to the front of the platform, the crowd applauded. He held up his hand for silence.

In his big booming voice, Crocker called on others, one by one, to speak. There were seven in all, and each man loved to make speeches. The audience was pretty tired by the time Governor Stanford, the last orator, got up. But he was their favorite and the Sacramentans went wild.

Governor Stanford was a fine figure of a man. He was as tall as Crocker and very straight, with a black beard trimmed in the height of fashion. He opened his mouth very wide and spoke loud and clear. His words rang out and there were plenty of them.

At last he got to the end of his speech.

"The people of Sacramento," he said, pausing between each word, "the people of Sacramento will soon see passing through these streets the busy denizens of two hemispheres in their constant travel over the great highway of nations."

With that the Governor walked majestically down the steps of the platform to the levee, followed by the group of dignitaries.

Then came the really great event of the day. While the band played, Stanford picked up a shovel and threw a spadeful of mud into a flag-decorated, two-wheel, one-horse cart waiting there. Work had at last begun on the transcontinental railroad.

"The governor's action," the Sacramento newspaper said, "showed that his muscles were in good working condition."

Crocker waved his arms in answer to the cheers of the crowd. Above the din he shouted, "This is the first shovelful. The work is going right on, gentlemen, I assure you."

Singing about the great Pacific Railroad, the crowd melted away into the saloons.

You may wonder where Judah was that day, and why the chief engineer didn't make a speech. Maybe he was just too happy. The work on the Central Pacific Railroad was really begun.

* 77

At first everything looked rosy. The mines in Nevada and Colorado kept on yielding fortunes of silver and gold. The wagon trains rumbled in and out of Sacramento. Businessmen in Sacramento could see that they would make money out of a railroad joining California to the bonanza mines. To them, the transcontinental railroad didn't matter very much. What they wanted was the miners' trade. It was good business.

But Judah didn't care about business. His idea was to see a railroad built from California to the East, and he didn't care how much it cost.

The Big Four tried to tell him that building a railroad was a business proposition.

"Quick and cheap and get there." That was their slogan. Let the future of the railroad take care of itself.

Judah had many quarrels with Hopkins about the bills. It wasn't long before he fell out with all of Stanford and Company.

Resigning as chief engineer of the railroad, he decided to go back East. In Washington or in New York he might find men who would support his ideas.

Anna and Theodore Judah took a boat to Panama. On the wagon trip across the isthmus Theodore fell sick. The terrible jungle cholera that had attacked so many pioneers before him, laid him low. Two days after he reached New York, he died.

CHAPTER 9

Crocker's Pets

THE GOOD SHIP "HERALD OF THE MORNING"
arrived in California on October 5th, 1863,
bringing the first shipment of rail for the building of the Central Pacific Railroad. It had come
18,000 miles around the Horn to deliver its
cargo.

The grading and the bridge building across
the level plain, east toward the Sierras, had
been going on since January.

On October 26th the first rail was laid. By

February, 1864, the road had been finished to Roseville, eighteen miles from Sacramento.

Judah was gone; but the Central Pacific Railroad still had his surveys. As quickly as the officers of the company could get money together, they went right ahead along the lines laid out by Judah.

A wood-burning locomotive had arrived by boat early in the fall. The "Governor Stanford," as it was called, had cost the Central Pacific $2,282.85 in freight, but it was worth it. As soon as the road to Roseville had been finished, tickets were sold and train service started.

Charley Crocker was Chief of Construction. After selling his dry goods store, he had gone to live in a battered day coach that shuttled back and forth over the line. Although he wasn't a railroad engineer, he seemed to have a talent for bossing men and getting things done.

Money was sometimes hard to get, but the railroad was a-building.

Then things began to go wrong. The Wells

Fargo Express Company and the banks in San Francisco were jealous of Sacramento. The great stage lines of the coast—The California, The Pioneer, Ben Holliday's Overland—didn't want their business to go to the railroad. The Pacific Mail Company and other steamship lines, the private toll road companies, all knew that they would be ruined if the transcontinental railroad should ever be finished.

Plots were laid and a whispering campaign was started.

"It's all nonsense, this transcontinental railroad talk," said some. "The Union Pacific at the other end has never started building; perhaps it never will. This is just a swindle to get the Nevada-Colorado trade. Those fellows in Sacramento don't intend to build any farther than the silver mines."

"A transcontinental railroad is impossible," said others. "Not even a wizard could finish a railroad across the great American desert. Maybe the Central Pacific will get over the Sierra—but

* 83

where will they go from there? It's just a get-rich-quick scheme."

Money for building slowed down to a trickle.

"I'd be glad to take a clean shirt and get out," said Charley Crocker.

To add to his troubles, he couldn't get laborers to do the grading and track laying. There was a new gold rush now—a rush for Nevada and Colorado. Men wouldn't work for wages when they could strike it rich.

The only men Crocker could scrape together —miners and gamblers and ex-convicts—would be loaded on a train in Sacramento and hauled to the end of the line. There they'd be given picks and shovels. After working at the grading for a day or two, they would disappear, carrying the company's pick-axes, shovels and blasting powder along with them. These men had only taken the jobs in order to get railroad passes to help them reach the diggings.

Then Crocker's Chinese handyman came to his aid. Every place that Crocker went, Ah Ling went right behind him. Ah Ling kept up with Crocker from morning to night and when Crocker rested in his private car, Ah Ling brought him his food and drink. Crocker told his troubles about the workmen to Ah Ling.

One day fifty of Ah Ling's countrymen piled out of freight cars at the end of the line.

The bearded six-foot Americans who were working there leaned on their shovels and took time out for a swig of whiskey and a good laugh.

* 85

The Chinese had pigtails, they wore big straw hats and blue linen pants. Their shirt tails hung out. Their feet were wrapped in woolen stockings, and they wore straw sandals tied with cotton strings. The biggest of them weighed about 110 pounds.

But American workers soon stopped laughing. The Chinese worked from morning till night and they never looked up. They could lift anything. They'd go anywhere. They kept to themselves, they ate their rice in their own cookhouse and they never drank anything stronger than tea.

"Let me have more of these Chinamen," roared Crocker.

Ships were sent to China and came back overloaded with sturdy little wonder men, all thrilled with the idea of building a great railroad. The newspapers spoke of them as "the Asiatic contingent of the Grand Army of Civilization," but everybody else called them "Crocker's pets."

Soon there were more than five thousand of them. The foremen, the teamsters, the mule skinners, and the skilled laborers were white men. They added up to less than a thousand.

Back of the working gangs trains began to make three trips a day over the already completed track. Businessmen in Sacramento stopped whispering and came forward with plenty of money. It looked as though the railroad were going to be a good thing.

It took another year to finish laying rails through flat country.

Then the Central Pacific was face to face with a new enemy—a sheer solid wall of mountain.

Let me tell you what makes the Sierra Nevada different from some other mountains. They are sudden mountains. They go straight up from the valley like oversized skyscrapers. They are steep and bald-faced. Only a goat can climb them. They seem to say, "Stop!"

Dangers had always lain in wait for wagon trains that tried to cross the Sierras. Many a party had perished in the snows of the Donner Pass, near the top. The American River canyon was a death trap for horses and men. Sometimes even a wagon with an eight-mule hitch hadn't been able to make the grade. Often one end of a rope would be tied to a wagon axle and the other end wound —or snubbed—around a tree. Then, with men pulling away at the rope and with mules grunting and straining, the wagon would be hoisted up and eased down the other side.

These were the mountains over which a railroad had to be built.

Judah's plan called for the railroad to wind up the sides of these terrible mountains. Tunnels were to be cut through the hard granite and trestles thrown across the yawning canyons.

Would Judah's plan be practical? Could the Central Pacific make it across the Sierra Nevada?

CHAPTER 10

The Trail at Lodge Pole Creek

ALMOST A YEAR AFTER GOVERNOR STANFORD had turned the first shovelful of earth for the Central Pacific, and about two months before that railroad reached Roseville, the Union Pacific on the other end made a fumbling start.

The ground-breaking celebration was held in Omaha. At that time, Omaha was just a little town, so there wasn't much of a crowd.

It was just as well. The Union Pacific was not really ready to start building. Peter Dey, the

Chief Engineer, was an able man, but the surveys he had were those that he and his young assistant, Grenville Dodge, had made back in 1859. In the years between, the Union Pacific had not been lucky enough to have a Theodore Judah working to lay out the road. New surveys had to be made and more information gathered before a railroad could actually be built.

As though this weren't bad enough, the company's Executive Vice President, Dr. Thomas Durant, had as his assistant Consulting Engineer Silas Seymour. It seemed that Colonel Seymour disagreed with everything that Chief Engineer Dey wanted to do.

Colonel Seymour rode a horse that the workers called "Knock 'Em Stiff." When he made inspection trips he piled his rifle and his poncho and his bedding on the horse. Carrying an open umbrella, he rode up and down asking questions. The friendly Pawnees made all sorts of fun of him. Even Indians on the warpath would pull their ponies and stop short and have a good laugh. As you can imagine, the Colonel wasn't very popular with the engineers whose job it was to build the road.

Dr. Durant was an odd sort of man himself, to be building a railroad. He wasn't an engineer and he hadn't been in business like the Big Four of the Central Pacific. He had been a medical doctor. Very early in life he had become interested in Western railroad building. You remember that it was for the firm of Farnham and Durant that Dodge had made the road map he showed to Abe Lincoln. The Durant of the firm was now the boss of the Union Pacific.

Dr. Durant dressed in great style. He wore a flat black hat and a flowing tie, a velvet coat and light gray peg-top trousers. When he went out to inspect the work, he picked his way daintily through the mud without getting a spot on his polished black shoes.

The laborers wore wide Western hats and checked shirts and high boots and carried big revolvers. They snapped their suspenders and spat disrespectfully over their shoulders when Dr. Durant came around. He was always giving directions in a highly cultivated voice and that wasn't very pleasing to the laborers. They didn't

Thomas C. Durant

know that he had a small pearl-handled revolver under his fancy clothes and that he could shoot well and straight. The fact is he was a regular dynamo and the Union Pacific probably never would have been finished at all if it hadn't been for him. Once he had the idea he never gave up.

At the ground-breaking in Omaha, Dr. Durant was master of ceremonies. George Francis Train, an Eastern newspaperman who was one of the directors of the road, was there too. He wrote a long, long poem and read it aloud. Everybody made speeches. Very few people listened.

As soon as the speeches and poems were finished, Chief Engineer Dey started building the railroad. Right away there were quarrels about where the railroad ought to go. Everyone could see that the work would be harder and that it would cost more than anybody had thought.

Dr. Durant decided to go back East and see if he could raise the money. Nobody was sorry to see him go.

Those who were left behind decided that they first had to get some good surveys. Surveying parties were sent out to draw up a really workable plan for the Union Pacific Railroad.

The parties were very small—only about fourteen men to each crew. Their equipment was put into a couple of covered wagons—and a good part of that equipment had to be guns and ammunition. The parties worked hundreds of miles apart in country filled with Indians and wild animals. Bands of hold-up men roamed all over. Some of the surveyors were robbed or scalped, but most of them fought their way bravely through bad weather, mud, deep snow, and human enemies.

The surveyors who explored the first part of the road—the part that followed the Platte River—had the best of it. Most of their adventures were among friendly Indians. One of the chiefs who came to visit them had even been to Washington and had received a medal from the Great White Father, the President of the United States.

Farther west the buffaloes were a nuisance. The buffaloes liked to scratch themselves on the

94 *

markers that the surveyors set up. They leaned against them and rubbed themselves and knocked the markers every which way.

Out beyond the Black Hills the Mormons helped the surveyors. They knew every inch of the ground for they had suffered through it on their trip westward.

But the really hard job was finding a pass through the Black Hills. These are the foothills of the Rocky Mountains.

You may wonder where General Dodge was all this time. Even though the war was over, he was still in the United States Army. All during the war between the Confederate States and the Union, the white men had kept the Indians stirred up, getting them to fight first one side and then the other. The Indians had lost a good deal of respect for their white brothers when they saw them shooting each other. Now, they weren't ready to stop their part of the war just because the white men said so.

So naturally there was a great deal of what they used to call "Indian unrest." This made it necessary for the United States Army to send soldiers and their generals to stop the trouble. Along with General Sherman and General Philip Sheridan, Dodge had been sent out west to "pacify" the Indians.

By a lucky chance, General Dodge was stationed out there near the Black Hills. He ranged around with small companies of soldiers looking for unfriendly Indians. Of course he always had a scout with him. General Dodge's chief scout was Jim Bridger.

Jim Bridger was a real mountain man. He wore buckskin clothes with fringe and his hair was long and flowing. He had lived in that part of the country so long that he knew it by heart. He could wriggle his way through anywhere. Although he knew all the landmarks, he wasn't educated so he never marked any of them down. He had them all in his head.

Early one morning Jim Bridger came to General Dodge and warned him that there was a band of Indians waiting for him in ambush.

"We can't go back over the regular trail to Fort Bridger, General," he said. "We'll have to make it around the mountain."

Cautiously the little band zigzagged around the hills. They skirted the crags and immense boulders. They followed Crow Creek here and Lodge Pole Creek there.

Dodge acted as if he were on a sight-seeing trip, so Bridger urged him to hurry.

"I don't want to play no game of hide 'n' seek with them Indians," said the Scout.

But General Dodge couldn't be hurried. Although he was still in the army, his heart was in railroad-building. He made notes all along the trail, watching closely every rise in the ground and every river bed. The Indians followed closer and closer. Time and time again, Bridger changed his route. After a whole day of hiding and running, the soldiers finally reached Fort Bridger.

Everybody congratulated General Dodge on his escape. But he wasn't interested in anything like that.

"While we were running from the Indians, we found the railroad route through the Black Hills," he said. "I was sure there was one."

This was the news the Union Pacific survey parties heard when they got back to Omaha. Not long after, there was better news—Dr. Durant had returned from Washington with the money.

In the meantime Peter Dey had grown more and more discouraged because of Colonel Seymour's treatment. At last Dey gave up and was replaced as Chief Engineer of the Union Pacific by General Dodge.

In his pocket the General had the answer to the riddle that had stumped the experts. He had figured out a route through the Black Hills by way of Lodge Pole Creek.

CHAPTER 11

Drill, Ye Tarriers

"Drill, my Paddys, drill,
Drill all day, no sugar in your tay,
Working on the U. P. Rail Road.
And drill! and blast! and fire!
Drill, my heroes, drill."

TWELVE THOUSAND MEN CAME TO OMAHA
to work on the transcontinental railroad.

The town that had once been a "handful of matchboxes" was now a busy railroad center.

* 99

There were blacksmith's shops and roundhouses and terminal yards. Steamboats chugged up and down the river unloading supplies. Mules, horses, and oxen plodded along Omaha's muddy streets. Locomotives puffed and panted over the new-laid rails. Alongside them the pioneers' wagon trains, bigger than they had been before, were still heading westward.

Now that General Dodge was in charge of construction, the Union Pacific was really a-building at last. First went the graders and the bridge-builders. Sometimes they worked a hundred miles ahead of the track, blasting out rock with black powder, piling up embankments with hand shovels and wheelbarrows, building stone culverts and wooden trestles.

Behind the graders and bridge-builders came the trackmen. As fast as the trains from Omaha could bring up supplies the trackmen laid down the iron rails.

Most of the men were Irish. They dug their way across the Great American Desert like terriers digging for bones—"Tarriers," they called themselves, since they spoke with a brogue. They sang as they worked.

> *"Every morning at seven o'clock*
> *There were twenty tarriers working at the rock,*
> *And the boss comes along and says 'Kape still,*
> *And come down heavy on the cast iron drill,*
>
> *. . . .*
>
> *And drill! and blast! and fire!'*
> *It's drill, ye tarriers, drill."*

Some of the laborers were emigrants who had just arrived from Ireland, but a good many were ex-soldiers. Some were from the Confederate Army, and some were Federals. They wore their castoff Army uniforms—blue or gray—all mixed up with the scarves and broad-brimmed hats and high boots and checked shirts that were the usual laborer's outfit. They were a colorful gang.

There wasn't any G.I. Bill of Rights in those days. Veterans had to make out as best they could with jobs. When they couldn't find anything at home they drifted out to Omaha and went to work on the railroad.

There were privates and sergeants and lieutenants and captains and colonels. All of them were tough, hard, two-fisted characters. Every man carried a revolver or a rifle, and most of the laborers were experienced fighters. Part of their job was fighting Indians.

Even without the Indians, living was pretty grim. The graders lived in tents out in the open plains. The trackmen slept in hammocks slung in box cars on the railroad sidings they had just built.

The track layers rolled out of their hammocks at dawn. Most of their water supply had been brought up in barrels. There was so little of it that not much could be used for washing. When the men found themselves near rivers, they broke the ice and took a swim. The life was just as hard as it had been in the army.

But the food was much better. The most important person in a construction camp was the cook. Some of them were men, some women, but black, white, man or woman, their popularity depended on the meals. A bad cook would be run out of camp at rifle point.

Breakfast was the best of all. There were platters of meat, potatoes, other vegetables, canned fruit, pie, and coffee. The men didn't have to count their calories. They worked them off before noon, and came back roaring for more.

The boss of all these men was General John Casement, and his aide was his brother Dan.

General Jack was most often seen in a fur cap, a leather coat and high surveyor's boots. He had a stubby square black beard. Although he was only five feet four in his stockinged feet, he was almost as broad as he was tall. His belt bristled with revolvers and he carried a long black snake whip.

Once when seven men couldn't budge a freight car loaded with rails, General Jack came along, put his shoulder against the car, gave a heave, and got it running without any trouble. The freight car knew better than to stand up to General Jack!

He could ride like a Cossack and shoot like

Gen. John S. Casement

Daniel Boone, and was always in the middle of every mix-up.

General Jack lived in a freight train made up of four large boarding cars eighty feet long. Two cars were used for sleeping, one was for eating and the fourth was a cookhouse. There were also some shorter cars—two bakeries, a butcher shop, a general store, a saloon and bar, and General Jack's office.

As soon as the trackmen would finish laying a section, up over the new-laid rails would come two locomotives, pushing General Jack's rolling headquarters.

General Jack had been in the Army and he ran the whole works like a military operation. Orders were given for track-laying Army style —by the numbers, as they call it.

Track-laying wasn't just a matter of laying wooden stringers on granite blocks any more. The rails were of iron, twenty-eight feet long, and each one weighed about 350 pounds. They were laid on wooden ties and held down by long iron spikes.

General Jack's system worked like this: Back in Omaha Brother Dan loaded cars of rails. Each car carried the same number of rails and the exact number of spikes needed to lay them.

Then up came the cars to the end of the line—as many cars as two locomotives could push.

As soon as the grading had been completed and the ties laid, the military operation began.

Once a newspaperman came out from the East to watch the Tarriers lay rails. This is how he described it:

"When the train arrived, the boarding cars were pushed as far as possible toward the end of track and a carload of rails unloaded behind them. The boarding cars were then drawn back and about forty rails with the proper number of chairs and spikes were loaded on a small car and dragged to the end of the track by horse power. Here a man put a check under a wheel, bringing the load to a stop. On each side of the car were rollers.

"Before the car had well stopped a rail was dropped on the rollers and twelve men, six on each side, took hold of it. At the command, 'Up! forward!' they raised and carried it to the

106 *

proper location. Then came the command 'Ready! down!' and it was lowered into place. Two parallel tracks were laid at the same time by this method, and in thirty seconds the rail road was twenty-eight feet nearer the Pacific Ocean. Before the clang of the dropped rails had died away, willing hands pushed the car forward over the loose rails, and repeated the operation, as fast as a man could walk.

"Behind the car followed a man dropping spikes. Others came after, tamping the earth under the ties, and last came the bolters.

"The moment one rail car was empty, it was tipped off to one side, while a second was drawn up to the end of track.

"A horseman riding at a gallop then pulled the first car at the end of an 80-foot rope back to the rail dump. There it was quickly loaded to go up front again. Every few minutes the long heavy train behind sent a puff up from its locomotive and, pushing the boarding cars and the cars of rails, caught up with the work."

At this rate the Union Pacific was a-building rapidly.

And all this time the Central Pacific at the other end was fighting the Sierra Nevada.

CHAPTER 12

Indians!

THE INDIANS DIDN'T WANT THE IRON HORSE TO come snorting and tooting right through their hunting grounds. They did everything they could to stop the building of the railroad.

For years the white man had been pushing the Indians farther and farther west from the Atlantic Coast to Ohio and Illinois, next across the Mississippi, and then out into the plains. The Indians had had enough of this and now

* 109

they wanted to stay put. They knew what would happen—it had happened so often before.

First there would be the trains and the loco-motives making a noise and frightening the birds and the wild animals that the Indians hunted for food. Then would come the settlers. They'd shoot the antelope for fun and to pro-tect their sheep and cattle. The sheep and cattle would muddy up the streams and that would be the end of the fishes. What's more, they'd eat up all the grass and the buffalo would die of hunger. Then there wouldn't be anything at all left for the Indians and they would die, too.

They knew that the Eastern tribes had disap-peared this way—over and over again it had happened whenever the white man came into Indian territory.

Before the Iron Horse went out into the plains the United States made a treaty with the Indians —they were to stay north of the railroad line.

This didn't help the red men. Almost all the

buffalo were south of the line. They couldn't go a-hunting any more. The government had promised to send food but it wasn't nearly enough, so the hungry Indians decided to do something.

As soon as the surveyors began to come along, the Indians attacked them. The surveyors worked in small parties and the Indians had no trouble killing or scalping them.

But when the graders and the track-layers came, the crews grew larger and they could defend themselves better. Every man had a rifle or a revolver and there was always plenty of ammunition on the cars.

At an Indian alarm the men would drop their shovels, pick up their rifles and go into action. Most of them had fought in the war and they knew how to spread out and take orders. In a pitched battle they would jump into the holes they had been digging and use them for trenches. Or they'd take shelter behind the railroad cars and locomotives and shoot it out.

After a while the Indians took to attacking the camps during the day when the workers were away.

Once General Jack heard that the Indians were planning an attack on a grading camp a

hundred miles away. He jumped on his horse and rode as hard as he could, so he'd be there in case the Indians came. Every now and then he'd stop and rest his horse. Then he'd mount and ride again.

Late in the afternoon a band of Sioux caught

sight of the General and started in pursuit. Arrows fell all around him. The dust and the alkali got in his throat and choked him. He felt the blood running down his face, but there wasn't any time now to stop. He jumped off his horse and ran along beside it, holding on to its tail. When the animal seemed rested he leaped into the saddle again and galloped ahead.

Near sundown he was in sight of the camp. The Sioux gave a war whoop, wheeled around and disappeared over the horizon.

General Jack came into camp and stumbled into the cook house, covered with blood.

The big fat cook-lady came rushing toward him.

"Merciful heavens, General Jack," she screamed. "Is it the Indians got you?"

The General grabbed her around the waist and gave her a great bear hug. "Give us a kiss, Mom," he said. "It's no Indian arrow. It's only a nosebleed."

When the men came in from work, General

* 113

Jack, his face washed, was sitting in the chow house, eating a supper of meat and potatoes. The graders were surprised to see him.

"I rode a hundred miles today," the General said with a grin. "But both man and horse are doing well."

No Indians attacked that night. They knew General Jack was in camp and, like the railroad builders, they respected him.

One day seventeen Sioux Indians under the leadership of Spotted Tail, chief of the Sioux Nation, paid a visit to General Jack near Grand Island, Nebraska. The chiefs were dressed in their finest breechclouts and headdresses and they were all riding. They had with them their own interpreter, Pat Mullaley.

Pat explained to General Jack that they had come to see how the track was laid. The superintendent was very polite and led them to where his men were working. Then he took his visitors through the cars. Every car was stacked with rifles. The Indians were impressed.

Before they left the camp, the Indians showed how well they could use their bows and arrows. One of the workers stuck a shovel upright in the ground sixty feet away. Sixteen of the Indians put their arrows right through the hole in the handle. The last Indian hit the shovel, knocking it over. He felt disgraced.

Spotted Tail and his chiefs were then invited in to the chow car and given a fine feast. This was really what they wanted, for all the Indians were hungry. They weren't used to the white man's food, and when the syrup was passed around, they drank it right out of the jug!

After the meal, General Jack suggested that he show the Indians how well the Iron Horse could run. Spotted Tail was invited to get into the cab of the engine with his interpreter. Then the other Indians lined up to race the engine.

At the word "Go!" off they started. At first it seemed that they were beating the locomotive. They gave an Indian war whoop. But just then the engine overhauled them. This was the end of the race. The Indians went away discouraged.

However, they did not give up hope of putting an end to the railroad. They went along the line, ripping up rails, pulling down telegraph poles, and thinking up all sorts of ways to stop the builders.

At last they thought they had found a way to stop the Iron Horse. They strung a rope across the rails. Sixteen chiefs on horseback, lined up on either side, held the ends of the rope as though for a tug of war. By and by along came the train. The locomotive whizzed right by, carrying the rope along with it. The chiefs held on for a while, but they soon learned that it takes more than a rope and thirty-two ponies to stop one Iron Horse.

CHAPTER 13

Men Against Mountains

ALL THIS TIME THE CENTRAL PACIFIC WAS fighting its way up the Sierra Nevada.

"Here I am," that mountain stronghold seemed to say. "There's a chip of granite on my shoulder. Come on and knock it off."

"Charley Crocker's Pets," those straw-hatted, blue-shirted, pig-tailed, big-hearted Chinese laborers, took up the dare.

Up the sheer sides of the mountain went the sturdy little men. They pecked away at the age-old granite. Like a man with a jackknife, they whittled out the road by hand. They pulled themselves up by the picks until they won a toehold. They were a thousand woodpeckers tapping away with their little tools at the mighty mountainside.

Have you ever watched men building a road? They work with powerful machines. Bulldozers on caterpillar tracks nose along steadily, uprooting trees, crushing rocks, pushing aside anything in the way.

Steam shovels open their giant jaws and scoop out a ton of earth with one bite. Steam drills rip out stubborn rock, or dynamite explodes it into pieces and hurls it into the air.

But the men who were building the Central Pacific had none of these tools. All they had were saws and picks and shovels and charges of black powder.

It was men against mountains.

Each tree had to be cut down, one by one.

Each rock had to be chipped away. Each shovelful of earth had to be loaded on a two-wheel cart and hauled off by a patient donkey.

Every bit of earth was precious. Cartload by cartload it was dumped into the canyons to fill them up and level out the grade. Many a fill was fifteen times as high as a man. If the canyons were too deep for fills, wooden trestles, or bridges, would be thrown across at dizzy heights. If a trestle gave way the first time, another was built. Up there in those virgin forests there was plenty of lumber and to spare. And plenty of Chinese workers, too.

Men who fired the black blasting powder had to stand close to it. The powder couldn't be set off with a long fuse like our modern dynamite. Once the charge was set there was nothing to do but run away—fast. Many a little man didn't run fast enough. Up he went with the sticks and the stones and the rocks, never to run again, never to see his homeland across the Pacific.

* 119

At that rate it took a lot of digging and filling and bridge building and men, to carve out a workable grade for the railroad up the Sierras.

Up, up, up went the hordes of workers, inching their way until they were nearly to the top. There the climb was so sheer that they couldn't pull themselves up by their picks. Charley Crocker spoke about this problem to his Chief Engineer Strobridge. An idea came out of their talk.

They sent men crawling around the mountain until they were above the place where they wanted to work. There they fastened ropes to big wicker baskets and "snubbed" them around trees.

Then two Chinese, hammer and chisel in hand, got into each basket and were lowered down the mountainside. Hanging crazily, they pecked away until they had scratched out a narrow ledge in the face of the mountain.

While they were working there, only a few

strands of hemp held them above a sheer drop of thousands of feet. Many a rope broke. The baskets would go rolling and bumping down the mountainside into the valley below, carrying the team of workers to certain death.

Through it all, Charley Crocker was everywhere, shouting and driving the men.

"I stop along wherever there is anything going amiss and raise old Nick with the boys," he said.

Once a month he rode up on his big sorrel mare with two bulging leather saddlebags. He paid the crews himself, calling every man by name as he gave each one a silver or a gold coin.

The summer passed. Winter closed in.

Cold winds howled around the high peaks. The snow fell. Steam plows pushed up the mountains. In the paths behind them came sleds, loaded with rails, with food and supplies, even with locomotives—anything that was needed.

* 123

The snow got deeper and deeper. Even the plows couldn't get through.

At last Crocker called a halt.

He shipped thousands of shivering Chinese laborers back to Sacramento, but he kept a handful of the hardier ones.

During the summer a tunnel had been started through the mountain. Deep inside, all through that terrible winter the little crew burrowed away.

The bunkhouses were buried in snow and the workers had to travel back and forth like earthworms, crawling through tunnel-like passages hollowed under the hard packed snow. Many a man spent the whole winter without drawing a breath of fresh air or seeing the light of day. Even rice had to be thawed out before it could be cooked and eaten.

The snow got higher and higher. Now avalanches came thundering down the mountain. They carried away whole buildings—and any

124 *

men who were unfortunate enough to be inside.

Spring came. Thaws set in. Avalanches came more often now. Crews in the path of an avalanche were swept away. Months later, down in the valley, they were found still standing, frozen stiff, with their pickaxes in their hands.

At last it was summer. Gangs of men were sent once more into the mountain to finish the work that had been stopped by the snow.

Before they had closed up the gaps, the winter was on them again.

But Crocker was ready for Old Man Weather this time. All during the summer lumberjacks had been cutting down trees, and engineers had been building miles of wooden snowsheds.

Inside these miles of drafty sheds the Chinese kept right on working all through the hard winter.

The years dragged on. For all the millions of dollars spent, for all the work and thought, for all the men lost, it still seemed that the Central

Pacific might never conquer the mountains.

Only forty miles of rail were laid.

The Union Pacific had finished six times as many miles of track laying. It looked as though the Union Pacific might be running trains to the California border before the Central Pacific even got over the Sierra Nevada.

CHAPTER 14

Hell on Wheels

WHILE THE CENTRAL PACIFIC WAS FIGHT-
ing the mountains, the Union Pacific was fighting human beings.

Right along with the army of railroad builders moved another army of gamblers, thieves,
and confidence men. Their business was cheating
the workers. They'd settle down near the end of
track and a regular Wild West town would
spring up. The boom in each town lasted about
sixty days.

* 127

Every time fifty miles or so of rails would be laid, General Jack would pull up stakes and move up nearer the end of track. The men's bunkhouses and the cookhouses and the supply depots and the company shops would be knocked down, loaded on cars, moved up the line, and put together again.

Right behind the westward-moving railroad outfit would come that army of bad men. They'd pack up their amusement parlors, saloons, faro tables, and casinos that weren't much more than tents or log cabins with canvas roofs.

128 *

Then they'd hoist them on to wagons, and drive up to the next terminal point.

Cheyenne, in Wyoming, started that way. It sprang right up out of the plains at the end of track. Overnight there were 4,000 citizens, most of them bad characters. The lumber for the biggest store was brought in from Denver, 170 miles away, and the store was put up in forty-eight hours. Lots sold for $3,500 and there was even a brass band in town.

The railroad supply camp was located in Cheyenne all one winter. In April when the grading teams and the track layers left to work on the railroad farther along to the west, the "rough element" moved right along with them. Cheyenne became a quiet little town of fifteen

hundred people. Only a holdup now and then or an Indian foray disturbed the peace. For a long time it was just a whistle stop. Then it began to grow steadily. Today Cheyenne is an important law-abiding railroad junction.

But some of the towns would dwindle down to nothing but a depot, a few shacks for a station master and his crew, some crumbling chimneys and a pile of tin cans. And there was always a new graveyard.

"Hell on Wheels," these towns were called in their boom days, and they deserved the name. Shooting and brawling and killing went on from night till morning. Every other saloon was called "Bucket of Blood" or "Last Chance."

Saturday night was the big night. That's when the men got their pay. The paymaster would come up from Omaha, driving in a buckboard with two horses. A guard sat beside him with a rifle in case of a holdup. The paymaster carried as much as $30,000 and many a time the road bandits got it. But generally the money came through all right.

The railroad workers came into town all slicked up in their Saturday best—black silk handkerchiefs around their necks, big broad-brimmed hats, leather jackets and high boots. It didn't take them long to get rid of their money. Promoters sold them worthless shares in gold and silver mines. In the saloons there were faro tables and card games played for high stakes.

It was a lucky fellow who had a cent left on Monday morning when he got back on the job. Many a one never got back. A couple of shots would be exchanged. Then there'd be a new grave in the little cemetery at the edge of town.

In Laramie City a bad man named Ace Moyer owned the biggest saloon. He made himself mayor and justice of the peace. He put in his brother Con as city marshal and a fellow called Big Steve as assistant.

For a while the Moyers and Big Steve ran

the town. They set up a "court of justice" and robbed people with fake trials or shot them and buried their bones under the saloon.

This got to be too much for the citizens of Laramie.

One morning a railroad superintendent came into town on the night freight car. He was hungry and he went up to the hotel for breakfast. The streets were deserted and there wasn't a soul in the hotel. Then Superintendent Wood heard a roar out in the street. It sounded like a mob. One of the waiters stuck his head in the door.

"Come on out on the porch, Mr. Wood," he said. "They're going to hang Big Steve."

A Vigilance Committee had been busy the night before. They had run Ace Moyer and Con out of town, but Big Steve hadn't been quick enough. Now the Vigilantes were hanging him while Superintendent Wood and the crowd looked on.

All this hullabaloo wasn't good for railroad building. It wasn't good for business, either.

As soon as a town became the terminus of the railroad, regular trains would begin to come in from the East. At the terminus, passengers and freight were transferred to the stagecoach bound for California. All the shooting and killing frightened the passengers.

When the railroad got to Julesberg, Chief Engineer Dodge called in General Jack. "You'll just have to do something, General Casement," he said. "I'm bringing some Congressmen out here to inspect progress. I don't want them and their wives to see all these goings-on."

"This town's the worst yet," said General Jack. "A bunch of gamblers took the land that we set aside for railroad shops and put up a faro joint. I'll use that as an excuse to clean up Julesberg."

General Jack got together a hundred seasoned workers who had served as soldiers. They swept down on the town. Then along the main street they went, from honky-tonk to honky-tonk. They picked up the anti-law-and-order men and marched them out to the edge of town.

Three weeks later Chief Engineer Dodge and his party of important people arrived in Julesberg.

The first thing General Dodge did was take General Jack into a corner.

"Are the gamblers behaving quietly?" General Dodge asked.

"You bet they are, General," answered the stocky little Chief of Construction. "They're out there in the graveyard. They all died with their boots on, but they brought peace."

CHAPTER 15

Meridian 100

THE PARTY TO JULESBERG WASN'T THE
first one that the Union Pacific had conducted
over the line.

Dr. Durant had discovered that Congressmen
liked to ride on the railroad, especially when it
didn't cost them anything. So every now and
then he'd organize a junket in grand style.
Newspapermen and men with money and of
course the lawmakers and their wives and friends

* 135

would be invited to come out and see what was going on.

The newspaper people wrote flowery descriptions of the trips. The financial men saw that the railroad building was going ahead and that made them anxious to buy shares. And the Congressmen went back to Washington in a good humor, reported progress, and lent a willing ear to the railroad lobby.

One of the biggest of the junkets took place when the railroad had crossed the 100th meridian, 247 miles out from Omaha. You might almost say that this trip was the beginning of modern advertising.

Of course Dr. Durant in his black velvet coat and broad-brimmed hat and French checked trousers was there. Senator Oakes Ames, who manufactured the shovels that the Tarriers used, went along, too. Being officials of the Union Pacific, both men acted as hosts for the party.

Among the visitors were Robert Lincoln, son of the late President; the Marquis de Chambrun, a descendant of LaFayette; and the Scottish Earl of Arlie. The Earl brought his valet. But almost everybody brought guests. Wives, daughters, sisters, and neighbors were asked along to see the wonders of the new railroad.

There were newspapermen sent from all the big dailies. The great Joseph Medill of the Chicago *Tribune* came himself.

The excursionists traveled in the new Pullman cars—by courtesy of Mr. Pullman. They were all agog over the mahogany-trimmed, red plush, gilt-decorated cars. They raved about the comfort of night travel in Mr. Pullman's new patent beds. Everybody wanted to try out the wonderful upper berths.

Those who lived in the Eastern states rode with Dr. Durant from New York to Chicago by special train. It was one of the first through trains to run between these two cities.

From Chicago the party went on to the Mississippi, ferried across the river, went by rail up the same little old Hannibal and St. Jo to the Missouri, up the "Big Muddy" by two gorgeous packet boats, and so to Omaha.

All along the route they were greeted by crowds of excited citizens. There were torchlight processions and band concerts and, of course, speeches. In Pittsburgh, Pennsylvania, where there still was no hotel, the leading citizens in the community entertained the excursionists in their own homes.

But all this was nothing compared to what happened in Omaha, which now called itself "the fairest town site on the Missouri" and "the threshold of the Great West."

"The beauty, wealth and intellect of Omaha" gathered together at a sumptuous ball. The Easterners met the Governor, the Secretary of State, the Chief Justice of the Territory of Nebraska, and the rich men of the town. Among these were a grocer who did a million dollars' worth of business each year, and a land promoter who had shipped ready-built houses from Chicago and set them up in a real estate sub-division.

138 *

The visitors saw the shaded homes on Capitol Hill and the new Capitol at the top. They stared at the cornfields that stretched away from the town, and at the roundhouses and shops of the Union Pacific.

But more wonders were to come. The excursion train left Omaha crowded with 250 people. Along with the travelers went the Great Western Light Guard Band, directed by A.J. Vaas, and Rosenblatt's St. Joseph Band. The cars that made up the train were the pride of the road. "Nothing that paint, gilt, varnish, velvet, glass, and the hand of the most skillful artist could do but was done to render these cars the most sumptuous and resplendent not only in Omaha but in the world."

"Magnificent dinners with the choicest wines and liquors were prepared and served under the direction of H. Kingsley, the Delmonico of Chicago." One menu consisted of forty-two items.

Lest the travelers become dull from all the

eating and drinking and speechmaking, the train paused more than once. The excursionists poured out onto the flat prairie, and under the wide Western sky they danced the schottische, the polka and the new waltz, while the brass bands played.

At one point a tent city had been erected. The friendly Pawnee Indians came into camp and treated the Easterners to an exhibition of Indian dancing and bow-and-arrow marksmanship. They showed their skill in riding and delighted the tenderfeet with imitation war whoops.

Of course the gentlemen of the party, and a very few ladies, went up to see General Jack's Irish-American army of track-layers. They saw how quickly and efficiently the work went on, and were full of praise for General Jack and his tarriers.

Dr. Durant didn't let a chance slip by to point out to the Congressmen what a wonderful job the Union Pacific was doing.

One day he had the visitors taken on a buf-

140 *

falo hunt. Indian Scouts and United States Army men joined the party in the sport. That night there was something added to the menu. Besides the two soups, the two kinds of fish, five boiled meats, seven roasts, twenty-nine entrees, eleven relishes, twenty pastries, sixteen desserts, tea, coffee, chocolate, fruit, nuts and bonbons, there was buffalo steak.

After dinner the guests who were able to stay awake played parlor games. George Francis Train, who had written the dedication at the ground-breaking in Omaha more than three years before, wrote another poem. It had 243 verses. Mrs. George Francis Train, described as "one of the most perfect ladies ever seen," read the verses aloud.

The guests retired early. They had to be up at the crack of dawn for their return trip.

The next morning, with bands playing, flags flying, whistles tooting, laborers cheering, and Indians whooping, they started back East.

They reached home full of good food and

good drink and tall tales about buffaloes and Indians and railroad building. Some wrote stories for the magazines and newspapers. Some made speeches in Congress. Some told their friends about it. Excitement ran high. They called it the Arabian Nights Entertainment of the Age.

More and more shares of Union Pacific changed hands in Wall Street. The stocks went up and the Union Pacific went right on across the Great American Desert.

CHAPTER 16

The Home Stretch

THE BIG RACE WAS ON.

The Central Pacific had crossed the Sierras. Now it was coming down the mountain and out onto the flat alkali desert. Track laying went ahead quickly.

The Union Pacific had come around Lodge Pole Creek and was eating up the distance across the Laramie Plains.

By this time it was just a question of where the

two railroads would meet. At first the Central Pacific had expected to go only as far as the California border. Later, Congress ordered the Big Four to keep going east until the Central Pacific railroad bumped into the Union Pacific coming west.

Each railroad crew of the rival companies wanted to lay as much track as possible. There was great competition between the Tarriers and the Pets. But the race for a mileage record wasn't only among the laborers—it reached right up into the top ranks.

Money was the reason. Every mile of rail

laid in a valley brought $16,000 to the company that laid it. Every mile of track completed in the mountains brought $48,000. With this much cash at stake each railroad company was trying its best to beat the other.

As the two rail heads got closer and closer together, Americans from coast to coast grew more excited. People who owned stock in the railroad watched for the latest news. The papers were full of the big race. It was written up like a great sporting event.

With the finish line in sight, the men who were actually doing the building worked at fever pitch. From the highest official in his office to the last water boy at the end o' track, all were like race horses, tense and straining to win.

In April, 1868, Vice President Durant of the Union Pacific at Omaha sent a telegram to President Stanford at Sacramento.

"Have reached Sherman Summit, Wyoming. 8200 feet above sea level," it said.

Could the Central Pacific top that?

In his reply, Stanford admitted that Central Pacific could not. "Seven thousand, two hundred and forty-two feet has been quite sufficient to satisfy our highest ambitions," he said.

The junction was bound to be near Salt Lake City, the first civilized center in the path of either railroad. The Union Pacific tracks had been laid almost entirely across the open plains and Indian country. There had not been a town of any size all along the way.

The Central Pacific had come through uninhabited mountains and desert. To be sure, part of the road had been through mining country, and there a town would grow up for a few months. Then, however, the mines would be worked out and the place would be deserted to become another ghost city.

The Mormons around Salt Lake City were law-and-order people, business was steady, and the communities were there to stay.

Both railroads wanted to get the Mormon business. The one that got there first would have the inside edge.

Every day tracks were laid faster than they had ever been laid before.

Charley Crocker's Pets bent their backs and laid 362 miles of iron road eastward in 365 days.

The Tarriers coming west put the miles behind them.

"Those Chinamen beat an Irishman?" said the Tarriers. "Why, one Irishman could do better than any three Chinamen!" They laid one mile, two miles, three miles, six miles a day. One day they laid eight miles.

It isn't hard to guess that nobody worried too much about the quality of the road beds or how long the tracks would last. The tie-layers placed the sleepers farther and farther apart. When the graders struck a little hill they didn't stop to take it down. They went right around it. The map of that part of the road looked like a snake going somewhere in a hurry—all curves and wiggles.

The surveying parties went right ahead into each other's territory. There were Union Pacific men almost to the California border. There were Central Pacific men a long way east of Ogden, Utah. It didn't make any difference to either railroad that the other one had already done the surveying in both places.

But it wasn't until the graders came along that the workers actually met each other face to face.

148 *

The crews came working from opposite directions, parallel to each other and only about 100 feet apart.

On the high ground were gangs of Chinese laborers with their picks and shovels.

Down below them were the Tarriers digging away.

As they came in sight of each other, all hands stopped work. Neither liked the other's looks.

They went back to work with murder in their hearts.

Then one day big boulders began to roll down over the Central Pacific embankments. The Tarriers below ran for their lives.

The Irish fought back. A blast of Union Pacific powder shot into the air. With it went a crew of Chinese.

Here was a game two could play. It wasn't long before the Chinese returned evil for evil. This time there were fresh graves on the Union Pacific side. After this the fighting stopped, but there was still bad feeling between the crews.

Everybody realized that the place of junction had to be set before the tough gangs of track layers started the war again.

Back in Washington the officials of both railroads were discussing the place of meeting with Congress.

While this was going on, Crocker decided to beat the Tarriers' record at track laying. In a single exciting eighteen-hour day, his men put down ten miles of rail.

Even with modern machines and tools, this record has never been broken.

General Dodge was at the exhibition by invitation. He wasn't fooled by the show. "They took a week getting ready for it," he reported. "All the ties were there beforehand."

The officers of the railroads had made bets on the outcome. The Union Pacific lost.

The rail heads were so close now that there wasn't any time left for the Tarriers to try to see what they could do.

This was the end of the race.

Congress picked the spot for the meeting. On April 10, 1869, the two railroads were ordered to make a junction west of Ogden at Promontory.

CHAPTER 17

The Golden Spike

"What was it the engines said,
Pilots touching—head to head——
Facing on a single track,
Half a world behind each back."

THE GREAT DAY FOR THE JOINING OF THE
rails came at last.

Not quite seven years before, Governor Stanford had turned the first shovelful of earth in Sacramento. Now men had laid 1800 miles of

iron track over mountain, across desert and plain
—spanning more than half a continent.

It was a miracle of speed—an engineering
marvel. Men everywhere had expected that it
would take more than twice that many years
when Congress had passed the Pacific Railroad
Bill in 1862.

The great day on which the rails were to be
joined was May 10th, 1869.

The place was a level circular valley sur-
rounded by mountains.

A "Hell on Wheels" town had sprung up beside the track—a street of stores and saloons
and dance halls, with all the good and bad men
that always followed along.

Workmen drifted in from all along the line.
Indians, Mexicans, mountain men, and a few
ranchers came to see the show.

The two roads stopped short only a rail length
apart. Between them all the ties had been laid
but one. A place had been left for that tie in the
exact center of the space.

154 *

Visitors to the show were disappointed when the morning of the great day was cold and bleak.

> *First it snew*
> *And then it blew,*
> *And then, b'gosh,*
> *It friz.*

But toward noon the sun came out. Even the weather bowed to the great day.

Trains came roaring in from the east and the west, loaded with guests who had been invited for this last thrilling junket. Ladies and gentlemen poured out of the decorated cars, and swarmed over the place. No one seemed to mind the sea of mud underfoot.

The excursion trains were shunted on to side tracks to clear the main tracks for the big event.

In from the west came a gaudy train of cars hauled by the Central Pacific's Jupiter—a fine 2-4-0 wood-burner, all red and gold, with a broad Dolly Varden smokestack.

In from the east came Union Pacific's No. 119,

dark green and gold, a coal-burner with a coffee-grinder stack.

Out from the Central Pacific's Silver Palace Car stepped Governor Stanford with a stream of notables from California, Nevada, and Utah following on behind.

From the Union Pacific train came Dr. Durant with General Dodge and top officers from the Army. The sun sparkled on the tubas and horns and trombones of the 21st Military Band that brought up the rear.

As the officials of the two companies met, photographers squeezed the rubber bulbs on their clumsy boxlike contraptions set solidly on tripods. There were no flash bulbs and high-speed cameras then. Each photographer had a crew of at least three men to help him.

In the early afternoon the two locomotives moved up to the end o' track, facing each other. The ceremonies were about to begin.

The last tie was brought up. It was made of polished California laurel. On a silver plate in

the center an inscription read: "The last tie laid on the completion of the Pacific Rail Road, May 10, 1869." The names of the officers and the directors of both companies were engraved below.

Superintendent of Construction Strobridge of the Central Pacific, and Superintendent of Construction Reed of the Union Pacific, picked up the tie and laid it in its place.

Everything was ready now for the last two rails.

Six of Crocker's Pets stepped forward, their freshly starched blue shirt tails flapping in the wind. These men were the heroes of the day. Seizing the rails, they placed them on the waiting ties.

Now the only thing left to do was to drive the spikes.

Governor Stanford, Dr. Durant and several other notables came forward. They carried silver sledge hammers.

Telegraph operators sat nearby, waiting to

flash the news of the driving of the last spike to waiting crowds across the country.

First there was a little speech-making. Governor Stanford and General Dodge, coached beforehand to be brief, each said a few words.

"Hats off," went clicking over the wires.

Then there was another delay while the Reverend Mr. Todd offered up a long prayer. The spectators shuffled and whispered, the workmen on top of the cars and hanging to the sides of the engines grew impatient.

At last the telegraph operators tapped out the words, "We have got done praying. The spike is about to be presented."

"All ready in the East," came back the answer.

Telegraph lines were attached to the silver sledge hammers so that the blows that drove in the spike could be heard over all the land.

Four spikes had to be driven. Two were of silver and one was a mixture of silver and gold. These three came from Montana, Idaho, and

Nevada. The last spike—the golden one—had come from California.

Governor Stanford and Dr. Durant were given the spikes and they put them in place. The first three were made fast by various notables.

"All ready now," went out over the wire. "The last spike will soon be driven. The signal will be three dots for the commencement of the blow." An instant later the silver hammers came down.

"Done!"

The words flashed out. The last spike, the golden spike, had been driven home.

The country was united from coast to coast by an unbroken band of iron rails.

The two engines moved up until their pilots touched. The two engineers standing on the cow catchers ceremoniously poured champagne on the last rail. Then they drained the bottle and shook hands.

The cameras clicked. The crowd cheered. The band played.

In San Francisco on the Pacific, a cannon fired a salute.

In New York City on the Atlantic the bells of Trinity Church rang wildly.

In cities all across the United States there were celebrations.

Some people who were at Promontory that day report that the crowd joined hands and sang "Auld Lang Syne." Others tell how bottles were passed from hand to hand and how good feeling ran high. Probably both were right.

A new chapter was beginning in the history of America.

The great Pacific Railroad at last had been completed.

CHAPTER 18

The Big Bonanza

NOW THE EAST AND THE WEST WERE REALLY
one nation. The ceremony at Promontory made
that clear to everybody.

The building of the railroads had opened up
that part of the country that lay between the
Missouri River and the California border.

Before the Pacific Railroad was built, people thought of that vast expanse as the Great
American Desert. When the surveyors and the
graders went out, it wasn't long before they dis-

* 163

covered that this wasn't true. There really was no such thing as a Great American Desert.

The Union Pacific and the Central Pacific had proved that a transcontinental railroad could be built. Long before the railroads met at Promontory, three more transcontinental railroad companies had made a start. A network of lines soon reached out into every part of that formerly unknown territory. Today there are five great roads crossing the continent.

Everywhere the railroads went the Wild West faded away. Trains brought excursionists who "ohed" and "ahed" over the wonderful trip they'd had and went back East to tell the home folks about it.

Settlers from the East and North and South poured out into the wide open spaces. Cities sprang up wherever the railroads went. The "Hells on Wheels" and the ghost towns were soon taken up by a new kind of citizen. Businessmen with their families and household goods came out by rail. They settled down in Julesberg, Cheyenne, Laramie, Grand Island.

The railroad companies sent agents to Europe who brought back trainloads of sturdy immigrants from Norway and Sweden, from Germany

and Italy, from Poland and Lithuania, all hard workers looking for homes of their own. Farmers, ranchers, sheep herders, and miners took up homesteads all along the right of way.

They couldn't believe their luck when they saw the riches waiting for them in the newly opened country. There was plenty of grass. In many places irrigation was the only thing needed to turn the plains into fertile land. Iowa and Dakota and Nebraska—that part of the country that Asa Whitney had offered to take off the government's hands at ten cents an acre—became worth many times that much, now that there was transportation. Today, it is part of the great wheat and corn belt of the United States—one of our richest possessions.

New coal fields were discovered—and copper and magnesium and even iron, and more gold and silver.

There seemed to be no end to the forests.

Most of the people who went out there got to work to build up the country. They carved a great empire out of the wild land to add to the United States.

But some of the new settlers went wild. They spread over the land like a swarm of hungry

166 *

locusts. They didn't take care of the soil. There was so much of it that people thought it would never give out. They planted it and re-planted it until it was no longer any good for growing things.

In a few short years greedy hunters almost wiped out the buffalo. Buffaloes run in great herds or stands. A man with a gun can creep up on them if he keeps to leeward so they don't get the scent. After one or two leaders are shot, the rest just stand there stupidly. A hunter can then shoot them down until his gun muzzle gets too hot.

One hunter killed 120 buffaloes at one stand in forty minutes. Brick Bond, an old hunter, known to be a truthful man, said he killed 1500 in seven days. Two hundred and fifty was his biggest day's kill. These men sold the buffalo hides for fur. They didn't bother with the meat that was so precious to the Indians. They just left it lying on the plains for the coyotes and the eagles. Later on, other men came back, gathered

* 167

up the picked bones and sold them by the carload for fertilizer.

Hunting parties were organized for sport. Noblemen from Europe, frontiersmen, and even women, rode on the buffalo chase. General Philip Sheridan and Buffalo Bill once gave a party in Nebraska for Grand Duke Alexis of Russia.

You can imagine that very soon there weren't many buffalo left.

After the buffalo were gone, thousands of heads of cattle were turned loose to graze on the prairie. Millions of sheep followed, nibbling at the remains of the grass until there wasn't a blade left.

The settlers and the farmers killed off the flocks of wild geese, the storks, the cranes, the swans, the ducks, the prairie chickens and the quail. By and by there wasn't even a wild turkey left.

Lumber companies went into the forests and

168 *

cut down thousands of feet of timber, and burned what they didn't use.

It was a great big party in the get-rich-quick spirit—the Big Bonanza.

The Indians were treated with little respect for their rights. If they resisted, experienced troops led by men like General Sherman and General Sheridan went out and "pacified" them. General Sheridan's slogan was, "The only good Indian is a dead Indian." Red Cloud, the Indian chief who had visited General Dodge, was one of the last to be put down.

The Indians who were left were herded into little reservations where there wasn't room enough for anybody to make a living. Even then they weren't let alone. If the white men found something on the reservations that they wanted for themselves—oil, for example—they got the government to move the Indians somewhere else —usually to some place even worse.

The more sober citizens in that section had

been trying to make the government listen to them for a long time. Before it was too late, they wanted the rest of the country to understand the terrible things that were happening to the land and the Indians. At last, frightened by droughts and floods and dust storms, people everywhere were aroused.

President Theodore Roosevelt, our twenty-fifth President, became one of the leaders in a new movement. It was called "conservation of our national resources."

Little by little, laws were passed against cutting down trees unless new ones were planted. A limit was set on shooting birds, and the government hired experts to teach people how to take care of worn-out farm land.

When Franklin D. Roosevelt became President, thousands of young men were sent out from the cities to the Civilian Conservation Corps. They replanted forests, set aside bird sanctuaries, built government dams for irrigation, fought forest fires, and put fertilizer into worn-out earth.

Just before World War II there were terrible wind storms. They turned the wonderful planting ground into a dust bowl. Men, by their greed, had almost succeeded in really creating a great American desert.

People have learned by this time that what a farmer does in North Dakota can make a flood in Louisiana. Conservation of national resources is everybody's business.

Even the Indians are getting better treatment. First they were made wards of the government. Today there are more Indians living in the United States than there were that day when Abraham Lincoln was in Council Bluffs with Grenville Dodge.

When World War II came, thousands of Indians enlisted in the American Army. They didn't serve as scouts or as a band on the warpath. They were G.I.s and officers like everybody else.

Fair-minded people think now that they shouldn't have to live on reservations, that they should go everywhere they want to, and be invited to become United States citizens.

Sometimes Americans are slow to wake up, but when they do, they really mean business.

CHAPTER 19

What the Railroads Brought

O N JULY 4TH, 1828, THE FIRST STONE HAD been laid for the building of the Baltimore and Ohio—the first public railroad in the United States. Forty-one years later, on May 10, 1869, the last rail was laid at Promontory.

Most people had forgotten the time when a farmer could set his load of hay on a couple of wooden stringers, hitch up his horse, and drive to the nearest market. They'd forgotten Senator Benton's plan to build a highway of rails owned and operated by the government as a national service. They didn't even remember the little locomotivators that couldn't go up a hill.

Wooden stringers were a thing of the past. Even iron tracks were out of date. Before the last iron rail was laid at Promontory, steel rails began to pour out of the rolling mills in Pittsburgh and Scranton and Wheeling and a dozen other places.

The gay-colored engines with Dolly Varden stacks, and the coffee-grinder coal-burning engines gave way to big black iron monsters—the Mikados and the Mallets—with as many as six, eight, or even sixteen driving wheels. These huge engines could pull trains of fifty to eighty steel freight cars.

Today Diesel engines click over the rails where once General Jack's men fought the Indians. A great gas turbine-electric speeds over the Union Pacific lines. Its voice, a high-pitched wail like the scream of a jet, echoes through canyons where men once chipped away rock with hand-pick and shovel.

All over the country, automobiles are run with Oklahoma oil, houses are heated with Pennsylvania coal, and furnaces made from Minnesota iron. Almost everything you use or eat comes from some distant place and, nine chances out of ten, it came as freight on a railroad train.

Anybody can sit down today in San Francisco, Chicago or New York, and eat grapefruit from Texas, strawberries from California, oranges from Florida, tomatoes from Maryland, and beef from Kansas. The meal can be topped off with Vermont cheese and Washington apples. This isn't a special party like the feast at the Hundredth Meridian. It's just an ordinary meal, delivered to you every day by the American railroads.

If you're ever lucky enough to make the trip across the continent by rail, it will seem to you that the corn and the wheat fields of Kansas, Nebraska and the Dakotas never stop. All through Colorado and Montana, cattle along the right of way stop chewing long enough to turn their white faces and look after the Iron Horse. They aren't frightened as the Indian ponies were. The cattle are used to seeing trains.

You go through big towns like Butte and Denver and Lincoln and Minneapolis that might not be there at all if it weren't for the railroad. Even Omaha would probably still be a "handful of matchboxes" out in the middle of what used to be nowhere before the trains came.

And when you get to California you are still in the United States, not in a separate nation that looks to the Orient and does all its trade with China and India or even Russian Siberia. When it was built, the transcontinental railroad brought California forever into the Union. In a California museum you can still see the Golden Spike that drove home the last rail—the symbol of that Union.

Much of the road that you travel over will be the same road that General Dodge laid out and showed to Abraham Lincoln. You'll see the grades near Ogden where the Pets and the Tarriers waged war. You won't see Promontory, though, unless you stop off and drive there, for now the railroad goes from Ogden out over the Lucin Cut-off. This is a causeway built right across the middle of the Great Salt Lake.

You will ride along the edge of the Sierra and look down the steep cliffs where Chinese laborers hung in baskets to blaze the trail. You will pass through many of the great tunnels where railroad crews spent their long hard winters.

You will be traveling in an air-conditioned train. The lighting will be soft and the riding easy. You can eat and sleep and even bathe and go to the movies in those trains. They are less gaudy than the Silver Palace cars of the early Central Pacific or the cars that carried guests to the Hundredth Meridian. But they are far more

* 179

comfortable. The central stove, the swinging oil lamps, and the red plush are gone. Old-timers used to say that when the Pacific Railroad trains stopped and started, the jerk would jolt a man's false teeth out of his mouth. Today's streamliners with their automatic couplers, ball bearings and air brakes, just glide along.

Seventy-five years have passed since Abe Lincoln picked the spot where the Pacific Railroad should be built. Many things have happened in that time. But the United States we know today would not be what it is if it were not for those brave men who had the courage, the nerve, the ambition to build that first transcontinental railroad.

It is a story of which every American can be proud.

Date	Date	Date
		returned